LIVING IN SPACE

BY THE SAME AUTHOR

LIVING IN SPACE

LARRY KETTELKAMP

MORROW JUNIOR BOOKS

New York

PHOTO CREDITS Permission for the following photographs or picture reprints is gratefully acknowledged: Boeing Defense and Space Group, p. 95; Martin-Marietta, p. 82 (art by Robert S. Murray); NASA, p. x (art by Alan B. Chinchar), pp. 6, 7, 9, 17, 19, 20, 23, 25, 27, 29 both (art by Paul Fjeld), 31 (art by Chet Jezierski), 33 both, 34, 35, 36, 40 both, 42 both, 43, 45, 48, 49, 50, 51, 57, 58, 61, 62, 64, 65 both, 69, 72 (art by Pat Rawlings), 73 (art by Mark Dowman), 75, 77, 86, 89 (art by Carter Emmant); Novosti Information Agency, p. 4; Teledyne Brown Engineering, pp. 47, 84; U.S. Space and Rocket Center, pp. 67, 68.

1 2 3 4 5 6 7 8 9 10

Library of Congress Cataloging-in-Publication Data
Kettelkamp, Larry.
Living in space / Larry Kettelkamp
p. cm.
Includes index.
ISBN 0-688-10018-X
1. Space stations—Juvenile literature.   2. Space shuttles.
Juvenile literature.   3. Space biology—Juvenile literature.
[1. Space stations.   2. Space shuttles.   3. Outer space—Exploration.]
I. Title.
TL797.K48   1993
629.4—dc20   92-35118   CIP   AC

ACKNOWLEDGMENTS

The author wishes to thank the following persons for contributing materials and offering helpful suggestions: Dale Andersen and Victoria Garshnek, Lockheed Engineering & Sciences Company, Western Programs Office, Moffett Field, California; Kyle Herring and Kelly Humphries, Public Affairs Office, NASA Johnson Space Center, Houston, Texas; Alton Jordan, Public Affairs Office, Marshall Space Flight Center, Huntsville, Alabama; and Christopher McKay, Solar Systems Exploration Branch, NASA Ames Research Center, Moffett Field, California.

CONTENTS

INTRODUCTION

Humans have always gazed at the skies, longing to travel out from Earth into space. The Chinese invented rockets in the thirteenth century, and military rockets were used in wars on land and sea in the late eighteenth and nineteenth centuries. But it was in the twentieth century that the way was found to actually send humans into space.

The American Robert Goddard developed liquid-fuel rockets in the 1930s and speculated on a practical way of reaching the moon. After the Second World War the German V-1 and V-2 rockets were brought to the United States and further tested

Space Station Freedom

1

and developed. When improved rockets successfully boosted the first Soviet spacecraft into orbit around Earth in 1957, the world suddenly realized that human space flight was also practical. Crash programs were begun to achieve this, with American President John F. Kennedy announcing the goal of placing men on the moon in the 1960s.

Today humans have been to the moon and back many times, crewed shuttles orbit Earth, and humans have lived up to a full year in space. Small space stations have flown, fallen, and been replaced with new designs. Through international cooperation a space station called Freedom is being planned and built. We have rocketed probes to the planets, and craft have landed on Mars and Venus. Steps are being planned to place people on Mars and perhaps even to change its climate so that humans can live there as we do on Earth. Eventually we may travel beyond Mars to other planets around other stars in the far reaches of space.

This book is the story of living in space, a story of remarkable achievements, goals, and dreams for the future as humans move out from Earth into the larger universe.

1

TO THE MOON

In April 1961 an important event took place in the Soviet Union. Six astronauts—or cosmonauts—as they were called in the U.S.S.R.—were gathered in the republic of Kazakhstan at a place called Star City. On April 8 one of them was chosen for a unique experiment, and on April 11 a rocket was moved to its launching pad.

The next day a message was broadcast by Radio Moscow.

. . . The world's first manned spaceship, Vostok, *was launched in the Soviet Union into orbit around Earth. The pilot and cosmonaut of the orbital spaceship* Vostok *is Major Yuri Gagarin of the Air Force, a citizen of the Union of Soviet Socialist*

3

Yuri Gagarin, the first human to orbit Earth

Republics. Comrade Gagarin withstood satisfactorily the take-off and injection into orbit and is now feeling well. The space-ship Vostok, *carrying the cosmonaut Gagarin, continues in orbit.*

Later Radio Moscow followed up with a report that the cosmonaut had landed safely after one orbit lasting 108 minutes.

Just one month later, on May 5, the United States launched astronaut Alan Shepard on a weightless trajectory into space. The flight lasted over fifteen minutes in a capsule named *Freedom 7*. On the 21st of July, Virgil Grissom made a second U.S. space flight of almost sixteen minutes aboard the capsule *Lib-*

4

erty Bell 7. Although these capsules did not go into orbit around Earth, they showed that the United States could lift humans into space as well. The space age had begun!

Project Mercury

This exciting race into space had actually begun earlier, with the Soviet launch of a small artificial satellite called *Sputnik* in October 1957. Three months later, in January 1958, the United States launched its first orbital satellite, *Explorer 1*. That same year the U.S. National Aeronautics and Space Administration, or NASA, was established to manage the nation's space program. The new agency began an ambitious plan called Project Mercury, named after the Greek messenger god. The goal was to lift humans into space to orbit Earth many times, and to safely return them to Earth.

The McDonnell Aircraft Company was asked to build twelve spacecraft that could be lifted into orbit by rockets and then recovered after a splashdown in the ocean. Later the number of capsules was increased to twenty. Each spacecraft could carry one astronaut. Many of the earliest missions were marked by problems and failures of the launch rockets.

While these difficulties were being worked out, test flights using chimpanzees as astronauts were being made. One of the chimps, named Ham, is considered the first "American" to make an extended suborbital flight; his trip in January 1961 lasted 16 minutes. Another chimpanzee, named Enos, made the first U.S. "manned" orbital flight in November of the same

Ham, the chimp, was the first "American" sent into suborbital space flight.

year. Enos was to go around Earth three times. But after he completed two orbits, some mechanical malfunctions developed inside the capsule, and Enos was brought back safely to Earth.

Three months later, on February 20, 1962, astronaut John Glenn went into space in *Mercury 6*, making three orbits of Earth. His flight lasted 4 hours and 55 minutes. Thus, only eight months after the single orbit of Yuri Gagarin, the Americans followed with a triple orbit. In May, Scott Carpenter

A Mercury-Atlas A rocket boosted astronaut John Glenn into the first U.S. space orbit of Earth on February 20, 1962.

duplicated John Glenn's feat with a space flight of three orbits in *Mercury 7*. In October, Walter Schirra doubled the achievement by going around the earth six times. And in May of 1963, Gordon Cooper made the last and most extended flight of the Mercury series. Boosted into space in *Mercury 9* by an Atlas rocket, he completed twenty-two orbits in 34 hours and 20 minutes.

Project Gemini

The U.S. Gemini program was planned to fill the gap between Project Mercury and later missions that would go all the way to the moon. Mercury capsules had carried only one astronaut. Their controls had been either automatic or governed from the ground. Gemini capsules were larger and could hold a two-person crew. (This is why the missions were named Gemini—after the star twins of astronomy.) Gemini astronauts had much greater command of their capsules. They could maneuver in space and control their reentry into the atmosphere.

In 1963 NASA ordered thirteen Gemini spacecraft from the McDonnell Douglas company. The first two Gemini launches were uncrewed. They tested the Titan 2 launch rocket, as well as the capsule's systems and its ability to reenter the atmosphere and parachute to a water landing. In March 1965 *Gemini 3* boosted Virgil Grissom and John Young up for three orbits. They controlled the capsule and the reentry themselves, proving both the worth of the craft and the skill of the pilots.

Gemini 4 carried James McDivitt and Edward White. During

8

Leaving *Gemini 4,* Ed White performed the first American spacewalk. The tether connected him to the capsule and held his oxygen line. White wore an emergency oxygen chest pack and carried a hand-held self-maneuvering unit.

their sixty-two orbits of Earth, Ed White left the Mercury capsule and went into open space for 36 minutes. This was the first U.S. "space walk," or extravehicular activity (called EVA for short). White was attached to the capsule by a tether, but otherwise he floated totally free in outer space.

In October 1965 an Atlas Agena rocket was supposed to be launched, but it blew up on the launch pad. This uncrewed rocket, numbered *Gemini 5*, was to go into orbit for a docking exercise. Instead, *Gemini 7* was launched on December 4 with Frank Borman and James Lovell. The *Gemini 6* craft that was going to dock with the Agena rocket was launched eleven days later. It was brought to within six feet of *Gemini 7*, and showed that two separately launched vehicles could rendezvous in space.

During the last five missions to follow *Gemini 7*, the upper stage of the Agena rocket was boosted into orbit to be used for docking practice. This rocket was called the Augmented Target Docking Adapter, or ATDA. First *Gemini 8* astronauts Neil Armstrong and David Scott, and later *Gemini 11* astronauts Charles Conrad and Richard Gordon, docked with the Agena rocket.

Crews on the later Gemini flights made many EVAs outside their craft. On the last Gemini mission, *Gemini 12*, Edwin (Buzz) Aldrin spent a total of 5½ hours outside the capsule. And, for the first time, the astronauts docked with the ATDA using their eyes instead of radar.

Project Gemini proved that a spacecraft crew could control all maneuvers and reentry by hand, could work outside the protective space capsule, and could rendezvous and dock with another craft in space.

The Apollo Program

When President John F. Kennedy spoke to Congress in 1961, he said,

I believe that this nation should commit itself to achieving the goal, before this decade is out, of landing a man on the moon and returning him safely to the Earth. No single space project in this period will be more impressive to mankind or more important to the long-range exploration of space. In a very real sense it will not be one man going to the moon. If we make this judgment affirmatively, it will be an entire nation.

The Apollo program set out to accomplish this aim. Named after the Greek god of light, healing, and the arts, its goals were to test equipment and train astronauts to travel to the moon, and then to land there, explore it, and return safely to Earth.

The Apollo spacecraft stood eighty-two feet high and was designed to ride on top of a Saturn launch rocket. The spacecraft had five separate modules, or interconnectable parts, within its cylinder-shaped shell. First was the command module, or CM, which had living and working space for the three crew members who would go to the moon and back. This was the only module that was designed to return to Earth after the moon mission. It was covered with a heat shield that would protect the capsule and then safely burn away during reentry into the atmosphere.

Next was the service module, or SM. It was the largest unit. The SM held a main rocket engine. This was surrounded by six wedge-shaped propulsion units that would put the spacecraft into lunar orbit when it arrived there from Earth, adjust the craft's course, and finally boost the astronauts away from the moon's gravity and back to Earth.

Next came the important lunar excursion module, called LEM or just LM for short. It was designed to leave the command module, descend to the moon's surface, and return using rocket propulsion. Since the moon has no atmosphere and only one sixth the gravity of Earth, the LM would also be able to operate like a rocket in reverse—it could use propellants to brake its descent. The LM also served as the crew's temporary living quarters while they were on the moon's surface, and had radio communications that were linked to the orbiting CM. In addition, the LM carried both still and video cameras; scientific equipment to measure radiation, tremors, and the moon's gravity and magnetic field; and devices to analyze lunar rocks and soil. In the later missions the LM also carried the lunar roving vehicle, which could be driven over the surface of the moon.

The last two parts of the Apollo spacecraft were the launch escape system, or LES, and the spacecraft-lunar module adapter, or SLA. The LES was an emergency device to eject the spacecraft away from the Saturn rocket in case a malfunction occurred during launch. The SLA was a cylinder that held the lunar module and connected the Saturn rocket to the Apollo spacecraft during launch.

The first Apollo missions tested the various parts of the spacecraft during launch, flight, and reentry. In spite of some problems, the Apollo spacecraft were successfully boosted into space and rescued after ocean splashdown, and the ejection system worked as planned.

Nevertheless one disaster took place during the developmental stage of the Apollo series. On January 27, 1967, three astronauts—Virgil Grissom, Edward White, and Roger Chaffee—were inside the spacecraft during a prelaunch test. A fire broke out in the capsule, but because the exit hatch failed to open, the crew could not escape and all three astronauts died.

While this was a severe blow, the Apollo program continued. During the test numbered *Apollo 5*, in February 1967, the lunar module worked well during ascent and descent. During the *Apollo 6* test a new entry hatch was installed. Although there was some rocket engine failure and the spacecraft did not go into orbit, all other systems operated properly.

Apollo 7 was the first crewed flight in the program. Walter Cunningham, Donn Eisele, and Walter Schirra went into orbit for 260 hours and 9 minutes. During their flight, they carried out a simulated docking in space.

Apollo 8 was the first crewed mission to be launched by the large Saturn 5 rocket. Lift-off was on December 21, 1968. By Christmas Eve, December 24, William Anders, Frank Borman, and James Lovell had approached the moon and gone into orbit around it. They returned to Earth after 147 hours in space.

Surveyor

Before astronauts could actually walk on the moon, many questions had to be answered. Some scientists thought that since the moon had no atmosphere, it might have a covering of dust several inches or even several feet thick. And whether or not it was dust covered, how hard was the surface and what was it made of?

To answer some of these questions and to explore landing sites, several robotic craft named Surveyor were sent to the moon between May of 1966 and January of 1968. Each was a triangular machine with a tripod landing gear that unfolded from the nose cone. Each landing "foot" ended in a circular pad, and each leg had a crushable block to absorb the shock of the lunar landing. Every Surveyor carried a main retrorocket and three smaller maneuvering rockets. A solar panel (for converting the sun's energy into electricity), antennas, TV camera, star sensor, and soil sampling devices were all part of its equipment.

Seven Surveyor craft were rocketed to the moon. The first made a soft landing in a place called the Ocean of Storms. It had come to rest in only one inch of dust, showing that astronauts would be able to walk there without difficulty. The second Surveyor crash-landed into the moon. The third did not turn off its engine when it should have and bounced up thirty-five feet, then took a second bounce of eleven feet before coming to rest. It dug soil samples and photographed them with a TV camera. The last few Surveyors in the series landed uneventfully.

The Surveyors sent thousands of television pictures back to Earth and verified most of the suppositions about the moon, including the nighttime temperatures of around −250° F.

Men on the Moon

Apollo 9 was the first test to include the lunar module. The capsule carried astronauts James McDivitt, Russell Schweickart, and David Scott. Two of the crew conducted EVAs in space and simulated a rescue of the LM (in case of an emergency during later moon missions).

On May 18, 1969, Eugene Cernan, Thomas Stafford, and John Young took off in *Apollo 10* knowing that they would travel to the moon and do everything but land. The CM went into lunar orbit, the crew practiced docking with the LM in orbit, and the LM crew took the module to within 50,000 feet of the moon's surface. After thirty-one moon orbits the crew returned to Earth. All systems were go for the mission to follow!

Though other Apollo crews had gone all the way to the moon and back, it was the *Apollo 11* mission that was to go down in history. The names of the crew members were to become well known around the globe as the first humans to reach the surface of the moon.

Apollo 11 was launched July 16, 1969. Michael Collins stayed in the command module to pilot it during its orbit around the moon, while Neil Armstrong and Buzz Aldrin used the LM to reach the moon's surface. Manually maneuvering away from a crater in the Sea of Tranquility, Armstrong brought the LM, code-named the *Eagle*, to a soft landing on the surface. "We're go! Hang tight, we're go," he said just before touchdown.

Armstrong was the first astronaut out of the *Eagle*, and the TV camera sent pictures back to Earth as he set the first human foot on the moon saying, "That's one small step for a man, one giant leap for mankind." Twenty minutes later Buzz Aldrin joined him. The two men explored the moon in their space suits, taking huge strides and bouncing easily up and down in the moon's low gravity. Armstrong and Aldrin ventured about three hundred feet away from the LM, gathered soil and rock samples, and planted an American flag.

The astronauts spent about two and a half hours as the first earthlings to walk on another celestial body. Then they returned to the LM, the *Eagle* fired its propulsion units, and the module rose steadily and redocked with the CM. The crew returned to Earth and made a safe splashdown in the Pacific Ocean. In only eight years the goal announced by President Kennedy had been reached, bringing new possibilities for space exploration.

In November 1969 another Apollo mission carried Alan Bean, Charles Conrad, and Richard Gordon to the moon, where the LM made a pinpoint landing five hundred feet from *Surveyor 3*, which had landed there in 1967. The TV camera and other units were recovered from the Surveyor. A special Apollo Lunar Surface Experiments Package, or ALSEP, was placed on the moon to gather long-term scientific data before the crew returned to Earth ten days after leaving home.

Apollo 13 was a near disaster. Some fifty-five hours after launch the crew of Fred Haise, James Lovell, and John Swigert reported a fire from an electrical short circuit. One of the spacecraft's two oxygen tanks failed, and part of its electrical power was lost. Six hours later the Apollo craft reached lunar orbit, where a maneuver was made to turn the spaceship around and

The 1969 *Apollo 12* mission landed 500 feet from *Surveyor 3,* sent to the moon in 1967. Astronaut Charles Conrad is removing the Surveyor's camera.

head it back to Earth. Although the CM did not have enough oxygen left, the crew survived by using almost all the backup oxygen stored in the LM, and tragedy was averted.

Apollo 14 was much more successful and carried extra safety devices. The astronauts were Edgar Mitchell, Stuart Roosa, and Alan Shepard. An EVA time record was set as the crew worked for a total of about nine and a half hours on the moon's surface. A moon-core sample was drilled ten feet below the surface, and a particle-measuring satellite was placed in lunar orbit. Even longer stays were made on the last three Apollo missions—15, 16, and 17. Each of these carried the special go-cart called the lunar rover.

Lunar Rovers

The lunar roving vehicle, or LRV, was powered by two 36-volt batteries. It could reach a top speed of around ten miles per hour, and the batteries could last up to seventy-eight hours. Like a dune buggy, the rover could drive over ten-inch bumps and crevasses almost two feet wide. It could climb up a moon slope of 25 degrees. The rover had two communications antennas, a TV camera, and storage spaces for scientific equipment and bags of moon rock and soil samples. The LRV folded up and was stored in a bay of the Apollo landing module, and then unfolded on the moon after landing.

Rovers were driven on the moon during Apollo missions 15, 16, and 17. Each LRV was used several times on its mission, the last one covering a record of twenty-two miles from the

Astronaut James Irwin salutes a stiff American flag planted on the moon during *Apollo 15*. The unfolded lunar rover is to the right of the LEM.

landing module. The rover used during *Apollo 16* actually televised the LM returning to the orbiter, ready for the journey back to Earth. All three moon rovers were left behind, and they can be used again during future missions to the moon.

The final three Apollo missions included astronauts James Irwin, David Scott, Alfred Worden, Charles Duke, Thomas Mattingly, John Young, Eugene Cernan, Ronald Evans, and Harrison Schmitt. On *Apollo 16* an EVA on the surface of the moon lasted over twenty hours. And on the final *Apollo 17*

During *Apollo 17* Harrison Schmitt and Eugene Cernan drove the lunar roving vehicle to this huge moon boulder.

mission, astronauts Schmitt and Cernan made an extensive survey of the moon's surface as they drove around in their moon buggy. The return of *Apollo 17* to Earth on December 19, 1972, marked the end of a human presence on the moon for several decades to follow.

In the space of the single decade between 1962 and 1972, America had boosted John Glenn into Earth orbit and, through the Mercury, Gemini, and Apollo programs, reached the remarkable achievement of placing humans on the moon and safely returning them to Earth. It was an impressive beginning in man's effort to conquer space.

2

LIVING IN SPACE

In the years after NASA sent astronauts to the moon, the U.S. Apollo spacecraft were used as part of a new experiment in space living called Skylab. Now the craft carried astronauts into space to dock with a laboratory in which they lived and worked, and then returned them to Earth. Thus the end of the Apollo program was the beginning of another.

But Skylab was not the first living laboratory. As the United States reached for the moon, the Soviet Union switched its goal and began developing a life-experiment module.

Created in the mid-1960s, this Soviet space capsule could be launched into orbit and serve as a life habitat. It was called Soyuz. Having been first to orbit a human in space, the Soviet Union had also planned to be the first to transport people to

Skylab in space, with "windmill" type solar panels of the Apollo Telescope extended.

the moon. However, the United States placed astronauts there first with the *Apollo 11* mission in 1969.

Meanwhile the Soviets flew five Earth-orbit missions with Soyuz in the same year. And in 1970 they kept two cosmonauts in orbit for almost eighteen days, far longer than the 94½ hours the U.S. had achieved during its earlier Gemini two-man orbital program.

In April 1971, the Soviet Union launched a larger habitat, *Salyut 1*, that might be called the first "space station." A few days later two cosmonauts were boosted to the station in a Soyuz

23

capsule. But they had to return to Earth because they could not open the hatch of the space station. Six weeks later three cosmonauts did reach the station and stayed in the Salyut module for a new record of close to twenty-four days. Tragically, on their return trip the capsule lost its cabin pressure and the three-man crew died before they could touch down.

Salyut 1 was removed from its orbit following the disaster, and the Soviets redesigned the Soyuz capsule for safer flight. After several failed launches over the next few years, the Soviets launched three more space stations between 1974 and 1976. Each was a version of Salyut.

As space stations go, Salyut was quite small, with very simple accommodations and a limited supply of electricity. It had only one docking port, which meant that each Soyuz crew had to bring enough food and water for the entire stay. Nevertheless this first space station paved the way for others to follow.

Skylab

As the Soviet Union experimented with Salyut, the United States completed its Apollo moon missions and then launched its own space station. In May 1973 Skylab was boosted into orbit. The Soviet Salyut had about 130 cubic yards of living space—the size of a comfortable two-room house. By comparison Skylab had over 460 cubic yards—about the inside space of a five-room house. It had two docking ports as well.

During launch one of the two solar-power panels was severed by a loose heat shield, so when Skylab reached orbit, the inside

24

temperature was too hot. Nevertheless, an Apollo spacecraft brought a crew of three to the station later that month, and they were able to fix the damage. This first U.S. crew to live in a space station consisted of Charles Conrad, Joseph Kerwin, and Paul Weitz. They stayed in Skylab for twenty-eight days. In July Alan Bean, Owen Garriott, and Jack Lousma took over and lived there for nearly sixty days. In November a third crew of Gerald Carr, Edward Gibson, and William Pogue remained for eighty-four days.

Skylab was built in sections that connected to each other. At one end the main docking port could connect with an Apollo spacecraft. Next came the much wider cylinder that housed

Scientist Owen Garriott performs a space EVA to place a dust particle collector on one of the solar panels of Skylab.

the rest of Skylab. It was made from the fourth-stage shell of a Saturn rocket. Inside the shell was an airlock module with its instrument units. Here inside air pressure could be reduced to match that of outer space. This opened into the large orbital workshop, or OWS, where experiments in space life and space science could take place.

The nine astronauts stayed in Skylab for a total of 172 days. The plan was that NASA's new Space Shuttle program would bring astronauts to Skylab for continued space-dwelling missions. However, the shuttle program was delayed. Sunspots, storms on the sun, caused Earth's atmosphere to expand. In its low orbit Skylab began to slow down from atmospheric friction. It fell even lower before a plan could be undertaken to boost it into a safe, higher orbit. In July 1979 America's first space station fell into the atmosphere and disintegrated in fiery pieces over the Indian Ocean.

Apollo and Soyuz Docking

During the 1970s the U.S. and Soviet space programs overlapped. The two nations decided on a cooperative space challenge. On July 15, 1975, the Soviet Union lifted a Soyuz capsule into orbit. Seven and a half hours later NASA launched an Apollo spacecraft. This capsule was basically the same as those used for earlier moon missions, but with an important addition. It had a ten-foot–by–five-foot docking module, or DM, that attached to the capsule at one end. The other end was built to match the docking port of the Soyuz capsule.

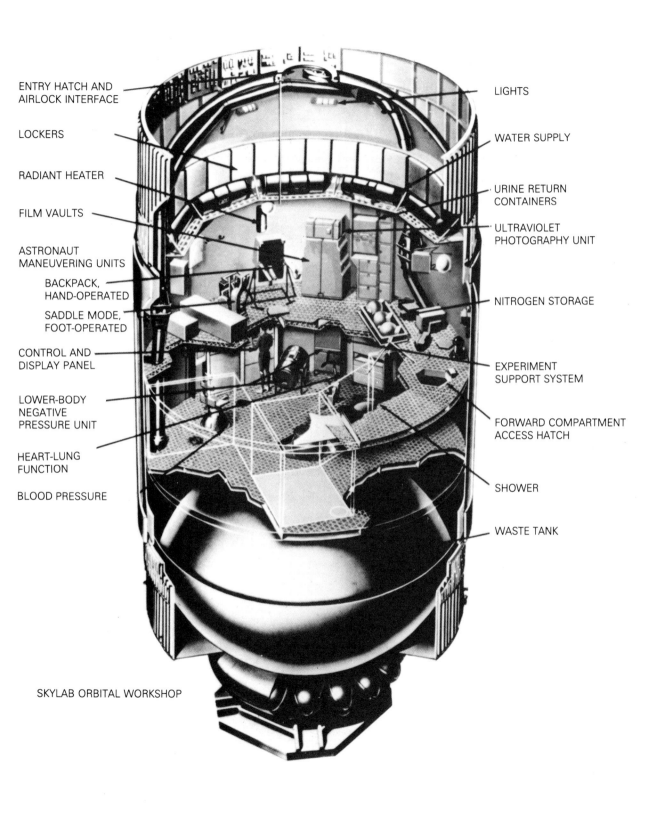

ENTRY HATCH AND
AIRLOCK INTERFACE

LOCKERS

RADIANT HEATER

FILM VAULTS

ASTRONAUT
MANEUVERING UNITS

BACKPACK,
HAND-OPERATED

SADDLE MODE,
FOOT-OPERATED

CONTROL AND
DISPLAY PANEL

LOWER-BODY
NEGATIVE
PRESSURE UNIT

HEART-LUNG
FUNCTION

BLOOD PRESSURE

LIGHTS

WATER SUPPLY

URINE RETURN
CONTAINERS

ULTRAVIOLET
PHOTOGRAPHY UNIT

NITROGEN STORAGE

EXPERIMENT
SUPPORT SYSTEM

FORWARD COMPARTMENT
ACCESS HATCH

SHOWER

WASTE TANK

SKYLAB ORBITAL WORKSHOP

Just forty-four hours after the U.S. launch, Apollo reached Soyuz's orbital position. Since the Apollo craft was more maneuverable, the main job of docking fell to its crew of Vance Brand, Donald Slayton, and Thomas Stafford. Three hours later Soyuz was solidly linked to the DM, and astronaut Stafford and cosmonaut Aleksei Leonov shook hands. The crews ate together, and each spent time in the other spacecraft. After fifteen hours of shared activities, including a news conference, the Soyuz capsule was released from the DM. A half hour later another docking was made as an extra test. Five hours after that Soyuz and Apollo separated for the last time.

Following the docking test, the Apollo spacecraft released the DM and continued to carry out experiments while in orbit. Nine days after launch, it began its return to Earth. It had a near-tragic ending, however, when poisonous nitrogen tetroxide entered the command module through valves that had been opened to equalize cabin pressure with Earth's atmosphere. But by wearing oxygen masks, the crew was able to survive until the Navy recovery team opened the Apollo hatch after splashdown in the ocean.

An Apollo craft successfully docked with a Soviet Soyuz space capsule after a simultaneous launch on July 15, 1975. *Insert:* During the linkup, astronaut Thomas Stafford met cosmonaut Aleksei Leonov in the hatchway connecting Soyuz to Apollo's docking module.

Space Shuttle

After the Apollo missions to the moon, the Apollo and Soyuz docking, and the fall of *Skylab* from orbit, the U.S. space shuttle program finally was underway. Its success depended on the ingenious design of a craft that could serve as a space capsule, withstand the heat of atmospheric reentry, and then land like a high-speed glider on a runway. About the size of an average commercial airliner, this shuttle became one of the most useful and flexible parts of the entire U.S. space program.

When ready for lift-off, the complete space shuttle looks like a large building with a stubby airplane riding piggyback on one side. The tallest part is an external tank holding liquid oxygen and liquid hydrogen as fuel. The tank is flanked by two rockets containing solid fuel, known as solid rocket boosters or SRBs. Each booster has an engine, while the smaller plane-shaped orbiter has a cluster of three main engines.

The SRBs provide most of the power for the first two minutes of flight. Additional thrust is gained by the orbiter's main engines, which use fuel from the external tank. Once the SRBs lift the assembly to an altitude of twenty-eight miles and a speed of 3,094 miles per hour, the boosters are separated and fall into the ocean for retrieval. The external fuel tank continues to feed the orbiter's engine cluster for another six minutes. Then the engines are shut down and the huge fuel tank is jettisoned, to fall back into the atmosphere and disintegrate.

The remaining unit—the airplane-shaped capsule we recognize as the space shuttle itself—becomes the Earth orbiter.

Artist's view of the space shuttle *Columbia* during its first launch into orbit in April 1981

31

It has three main sections. First is the flight deck on the upper level of the nose end. This is where the pilot and commander sit side by side and control the mission. During launch two other astronauts sit behind the pilot and commander on the flight deck. Three other crew members are in the mid-deck unit during launch. The mid deck is below the flight deck. It holds everything the crew needs for living: a galley for preparing food, sleep stations, a toilet, and storage lockers. The mid deck has a side hatch so the crew can pass into and out of the orbiter. To the rear of the mid deck is a special airlock module and hatch. This is where the astronauts put on spacesuits and special equipment for extravehicular activities. Behind this is a large tank-shaped cargo bay. The cargo doors can open directly to outer space. On one side of this bay is a robotic arm, called the remote manipulator system, or RMS. It is operated from the rear of the flight deck. It extends up to fifty feet and can move anything from satellites to astronauts into various positions inside and outside of the cargo bay.

The cargo bay of the shuttle is about the size of a large bus. It is able to hold everything from weather satellites to giant telescopes that are to be released into orbit, rescued from orbit, or brought into the bay for repairs in space. This area is an ideal size for a compact living and experiment module called Spacelab. With the addition of this laboratory, the shuttle is transformed into an orbiting space station.

The pressurized atmosphere is balanced in the flight deck, mid deck, and Spacelab so that the seven crew members can move from place to place freely. In Earth orbit the shuttle

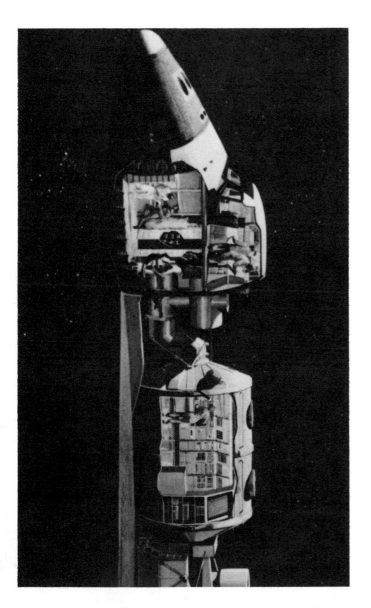

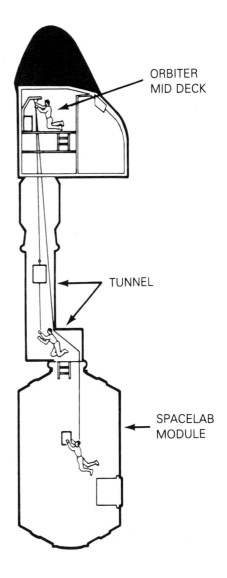

ORBITER
MID DECK

TUNNEL

SPACELAB
MODULE

This cutaway shows Spacelab connected to the mid deck of the space
shuttle. Crew members can move freely from flight deck to mid deck, and
through the tunnel to Spacelab.

appears to ride upside down. But of course whatever position it takes, there is no gravity inside, so there is literally no up or down. Crew members float about just by pushing off gently from one surface to another.

When a shuttle mission is complete, the orbiter becomes a reentry capsule. Insulating ceramic tiles cover the underside of the orbiter and the bottoms of the wings to dissipate the

An illustration of the space shuttle as its robotic arm releases a Tracking and Data Relay Satellite into orbit. Other spacecraft are pictured in the background.

On February 7, 1984, astronaut Bruce McCandless makes the first completely free EVA from the space shuttle using his manned maneuvering unit.

heat of atmospheric friction. Following reentry, the shuttle can fly like a glider and land safely on long runways built especially for it.

Space Transportation

The U.S. shuttle program is officially known as the Space Transportation System, or STS. The first orbiter was built by Rockwell International for testing in 1977. It was called the *Enterprise* after the famous spacecraft in the *Star Trek* TV series. This first shuttle was carried on the back of a Boeing 747 transport plane. It was released in the air and then guided to a gliding landing by C. Gordon Fullerton and

Teachers Christa McAuliffe (left) and Barbara Morgan (right) experience zero G during astronaut training.

Fred Haise. *Enterprise* was tested in rocket launches from Florida's Kennedy Space Center in May 1979.

The orbiter named *Columbia* was the first to be used for actual space flight. After many tests and revisions, *Columbia* made an orbital flight in April 1981. The number of missions now totals more than fifty.

The goal of the STS program was to have a group of orbiters, so that one would be ready for a mission while another was being maintained, repaired, ferried, or refitted. Besides *Enterprise* and *Columbia,* the other orbiters were *Challenger, Discovery,* and *Atlantis.*

The STS program was highly successful until the launch of *Challenger* on January 28, 1986. Because one of the crew members was a teacher named Sharon Christa McAuliffe, there was special interest among educators. TV sets in schools across the nation were tuned to the NASA launch at Kennedy Space Center. No sooner had the shuttle lifted off than something went terribly wrong. The shuttle veered off course as smoke trailed from the engines. Seconds later the shuttle exploded, and all aboard were killed. The accident was so devastating that there were no STS flights for the next three years.

Commander Francis (Dick) Scobee was one of the crew killed in the launch explosion of *Challenger*. A few weeks before the accident he had been interviewed by *Science and Children* magazine. During the interview he explained what it felt like to travel in space.

He described a shuttle launch as being "a bit like being on a runaway railroad train . . . the shuttle bangs and shakes, but we are still able to read our instruments." When asked about weightlessness, he said, "If you've never been in space before, the tendency is to try to swim to get where you want to go. We learn to push ourselves off gently toward something we can hold on to. After a few days . . . we are no longer afraid to dive headfirst down through the hatch to the mid deck."

Scobee described sleeping in space as like being on the world's greatest waterbed except that the astronauts' arms float out in front if they aren't tucked into the sleeping bag.

In the interview Dick Scobee also described the view of space from the orbiting shuttle. He explained that the stars look smaller and don't twinkle. The moon appears more gray than it does from Earth, and the sun is a bright ball that hurts your eyes. According to Scobee, ". . . you can see right down into the eyes of hurricanes and watch flashes of lightning in thunderstorms more spectacular than any fireworks display. . . ."

Toward the end of the interview Commander Scobee was asked if he would want to live in space rather than just visit. Scobee responded, "The space environment feels comfortable and like a place where human beings are destined to live. It feels natural to me to live in space, and I'm all for it."

Life Sciences

Before astronauts spent long periods of time in space, scientists were worried about how the human body would react. Some doctors feared serious medical problems or disorientation would result. The first U.S. astronauts spent about one and a half days alone in the tiny Mercury capsules. The space was very cramped, but no worse than the cockpits of many airplanes and gliders. They returned to Earth in relatively good condition considering the stress of atmospheric reentry and parachute splashdown in the ocean. Although they lost some weight and tended to feel light-headed after they returned to Earth, the effects were minor and of short duration, and medical scientists became more optimistic about the ability of humans to adapt to space.

During the Gemini missions, astronauts tested life-support systems and space gear outside the capsules, along with the effects of tumbling freely in open space. After the crews returned to Earth, doctors measured some very small temporary loss of bone density and muscle mass. And occasionally a few astronauts experienced some motion sickness like that in a car or boat. For the most part, though, there was little problem in adapting first to zero gravity (zero G) and then to Earth gravity again upon return from orbital flight.

The first detailed measurements of humans' reaction to space were made in Skylab, which had more space for equipment, and where astronauts stayed in zero G for up to eighty-four days. Doctors began to isolate the small changes in heart, muscles, bones, and blood cells. But the Skylab program lasted for only three missions—a total of just 172 days of space living among the three crews.

Between the time when Skylab dropped from orbit and the shuttle program started, life scientists devised a plan to study the effects of space living on various parts and systems of the body, as well as on the human personality.

In most of the early missions on the shuttle, the modular laboratory was used to conduct experiments in astronomy and materials science, along with a few life-sciences tests. Space Life Science 1 (SLS-1) was the first shuttle mission to convert the Spacelab module into a complete biological research facility. Instruments usually found only in laboratories on Earth were mounted into twelve racks running from floor to ceiling along each side of the module, in fourteen overhead lockers, and along the center aisle.

Four SLS-1 experiments had been developed to study the

Above: Pine seedlings grown on a Spacelab mission

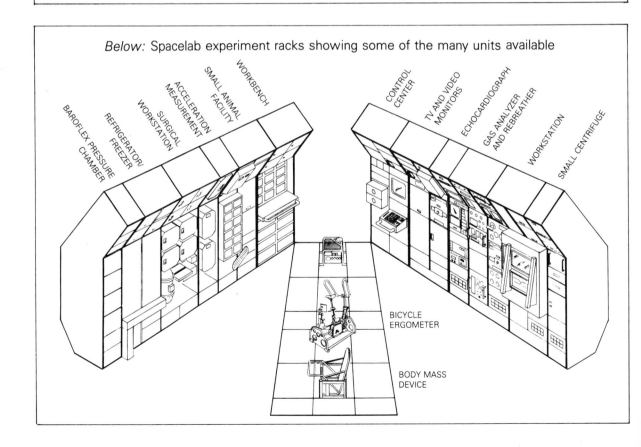

Below: Spacelab experiment racks showing some of the many units available

BAROFLEX PRESSURE CHAMBER

REFRIGERATOR/ FREEZER

SURGICAL WORKSTATION

ACCELERATION MEASUREMENT

SMALL ANIMAL FACILITY

WORKBENCH

CONTROL CENTER

TV AND VIDEO MONITORS

ECHOCARDIOGRAPH

GAS ANALYZER AND REBREATHER

WORKSTATION

SMALL CENTRIFUGE

BICYCLE ERGOMETER

BODY MASS DEVICE

effects of Spacelab flight on humans. Tests and measurements were made before, during, and after each mission. The first group of tests monitored an astronaut's heart and circulation. Before the mission, a thin plastic catheter was experimentally inserted into a vein in the arm and moved along the vein to a point near the heart. A monitor registered blood-pressure changes. Then during the first twenty-four hours of flight, pressure changes continued to be measured as the astronaut adapted to space. A second test for circulation measured blood pressure and blood flow in the leg. Legs may shrink slightly as blood and fluids leave the lower part of the body during zero G.

The heart was examined with an echocardiograph. High-frequency sound bounces off the various sections of the heart and onto a receiver that creates a moving image on a video screen. Early tests show that the heart tends to shrink somewhat in size after its work load is reduced in zero G.

A device called a rebreather also gives valuable information. One type is used along with an exerciser called a bicycle ergometer. Tests are made while the astronaut is both resting on the bike and actively pedaling. He or she breathes into the rebreather, which measures the amount of oxygen used and carbon dioxide released from the lungs.

Still another device used on SLS-1 was a pressure-sensitive collar called a baroflex. On Earth, changes in circulation occur when a person stands up. Gravity pulls blood into the lower body, creating an imbalance. If this is not corrected, the amount of blood that flows to the brain decreases and the person feels faint. But pressure receptors in the arteries that deliver blood

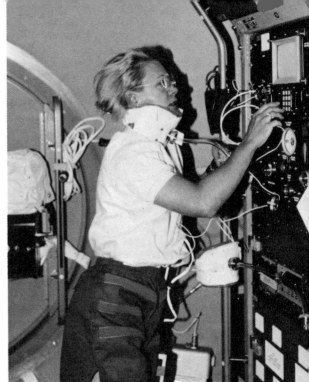

Left: Mission Specialist Guion Bluford takes a medical test while using a treadmill exerciser on a space shuttle transportation mission. *Right:* Mission Specialist M. Rhea Seddon wears the baroflex neck-pressure chamber, which is used to measure changes in blood flow to the head in zero G.

from the heart to the head come into play. When neck-artery pressure decreases, the nervous system automatically signals veins in the lower body to constrict. The neck vessels dilate, and the heart pumps faster to boost blood flow upward. This does not happen in microgravity, and the baroflex collar can measure these differences.

There are several ways to reduce the bodily changes caused by zero G. One is the Lower-Body Negative Pressure Unit, or LBNP for short. This is a suction compartment with an airtight belt worn around the waist. An astronaut climbs halfway into the LBNP. Some air is pumped out of it, much like a giant vacuum cleaner. The suction action expands tissues in the lower half of the astronaut's body, and fluids rush in just as they do in the presence of gravity. The LBNP is used on space flights to counteract long periods of weightlessness and just before astronauts return to Earth to recondition the body's systems to Earth gravity.

Astronaut Bonnie Dunbar is tested in the in-flight Lower-Body Negative Pressure Unit as researchers review mission procedures with her.

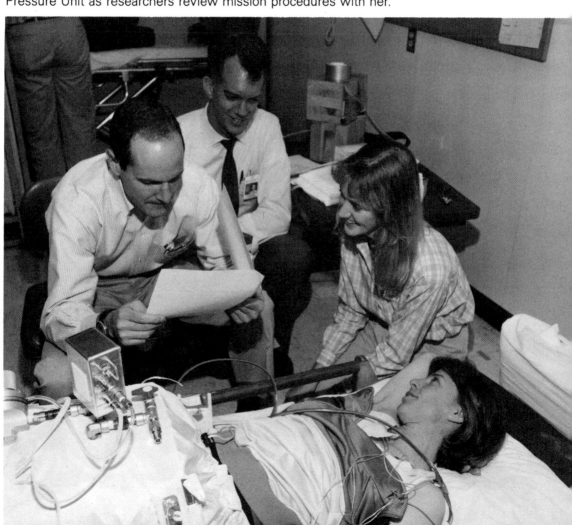

Another way of imitating gravity is with a centrifuge. If you have ever been on an amusement-park ride that swings you in a circle, you have been in a centrifuge. You sit at the end of the rotating arm and are forced against the back of the seat. As this artificial force, or G force, on your body increases, you feel squashed, as if someone is pushing on your chest.

In a centrifuge rotating in the zero gravity of space, if you positioned your body so that your feet were planted against the inside of the rotating rim, you would feel as if you were standing on Earth with its downward pull of gravity. If the centrifuge were large enough, it could supply artificial gravity for an orbiting space station.

Life-science missions aboard Spacelab are paving the way for more ambitious ventures into space. On the twentieth anniversary of the *Apollo 11* landing on the moon in July 1989, U.S. President George Bush spoke from the steps of the National Air and Space Museum in Washington, D.C. The president said, "We must commit ourselves anew to a sustained program of manned exploration of the solar system and—yes—the permanent settlement of space. We must commit ourselves to a future where Americans and citizens of all nations will live and work in space."

The president continued, "I'm proposing a long-range, continuing commitment. First, for the coming decade . . . Space Station Freedom—our critical next step in all our space endeavors. And next—for the new century—back to the moon . . . and this time, back to stay. And then . . . a manned mission to Mars. Each mission should—and will—lay the groundwork for the next."

The first plans for an elaborate space station called Freedom were proposed by NASA in the 1980s. It is an international project that includes equipment supplied by the United States, the European Space Agency, Japan, and Canada.

A diagram of an early proposal for a U.S. space station, showing living and work modules, solar panel arrays, a shuttle docking port, and a free-flying vehicle.

SOLAR PANELS

ROBOTIC ARM

RADIATORS

CREWED MODULES

FREE-FLYING VEHICLE

SHUTTLE DOCKING IN PORT

While the plans for Space Station Freedom were being studied, the Soviet Union was expanding its own space-habitat ventures. One of the Soviet goals had always been to keep humans aloft for extended stays in space. The crew of *Salyut 6* was in orbit for ninety-six days, breaking the U.S. record of eighty-four days made by the last crew of Skylab. Soviet crews that followed *Salyut 6* remained in space for longer and longer periods. The final Salyut record was 237 days, or around eight months, of uninterrupted time in outer space.

With *Salyut 7*, the Soviets used a redesigned Soyuz capsule. Four flights were made to test a new all-purpose craft that could be used as a ferry. It could reposition satellites and other craft in space, and could be used to tow new sections to the Salyut space capsule.

In February of 1986, a new Soviet space station called MIR was launched into orbit. From the outside it looks somewhat like a Salyut with larger solar panels for converting the sun's energy to electricity. But inside, it is far more advanced. Most of the life-support systems are run by computer. Communications are also much broader. Cosmonauts can contact ground stations and special tracking ships directly or through orbiting satellites. MIR also has six docking ports, so that as many as six spacecraft can be attached to the space station at one time.

In 1987 the Soviets expanded the space station by adding a science module called *Kvant*. This holds a group of rotating gyros similar to those used to guide airplanes or ships at sea. A gyro rotates at such a high speed that it remains in a fixed orientation in space. The special gyros in *Kvant* help keep the

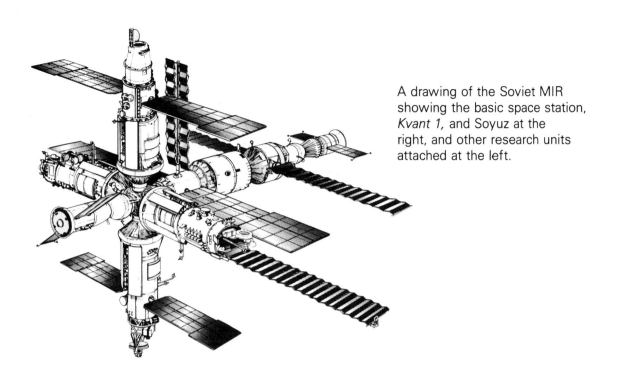

A drawing of the Soviet MIR showing the basic space station, *Kvant 1,* and Soyuz at the right, and other research units attached at the left.

space station MIR in a stable orbit or readjust the direction in which it is pointing. By the middle of 1990 two more science and technology units had been added to MIR, named *Kvant 2* and *Kristall.*

As space projects become more ambitious, they attract international cooperation. Equipment for MIR has been developed in several countries outside the U.S.S.R.; and visitors to the space station have included cosmonauts or astronauts from many countries, including France, Syria, Afghanistan, Vietnam, Mongolia, Germany, the United Kingdom, and Cuba. Plans call for U.S. astronauts to visit MIR in 1993 or 1994.

While there were many short-term crews and visitors, the Soviets continued to keep two-person crews in MIR for longer and longer periods of time. In December 1989 two cosmonauts,

Vladimir Titov and Musa Manarov, returned to Earth after staying for a full year on space station MIR.

Freedom

In 1991 the U.S. Congress asked NASA to submit a revised plan for its Space Station Freedom. This plan sets the stage for building and orbiting the station through the 1990s. The new design of Freedom is smaller than was first proposed. As redesigned, Freedom's overall width has been reduced from 493

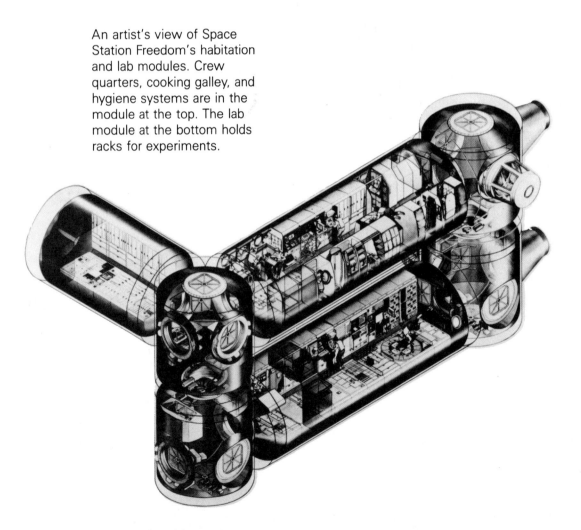

An artist's view of Space Station Freedom's habitation and lab modules. Crew quarters, cooking galley, and hygiene systems are in the module at the top. The lab module at the bottom holds racks for experiments.

This painting shows Space Station Freedom at the tended stage. The shuttle is docked, cargo doors are open, and the robotic arm is deployed.

feet to 353 feet. There are two U.S. modules: one is a lab, and one is living quarters. About 40 percent shorter than originally planned, each is twenty-seven feet long and fourteen and a half feet in diameter. Each module can be equipped on the ground and then transported in the cargo bay of the space shuttle. The basic U.S. lab module will hold twenty-four experiment racks, each eight feet wide. With the addition of future modules, the available racks will total as many as forty-five.

The first section of the space station is to be launched between January and March of 1996. The station will become "human-tended" in 1997, and permanently staffed by the year 2000. During the tended phase astronauts will be carried up to Freedom in six shuttle trips, and will stay and work for two-week periods. When Freedom is permanently inhabited in

An artist's view of Freedom at the permanently crewed stage. U.S., European, and Japanese lab modules are in place, along with the U.S. habitation module with a permanent crew of four.

This painting shows Space Station Freedom expanded to include box-shaped hangars at the top that could store a space vehicle or satellites. An Orbital Maneuvering Vehicle nears the station at the left.

2000, a live-in crew of four will be constantly aboard. Three sets of solar panels will be furnishing sixty-five kilowatts of electrical power for both lab and housekeeping needs. It is expected that seventeen shuttle visits will be needed to reach the permanently inhabited level. At the same time, an Assured Crew Return Vehicle will have been tested and docked at the station to bring crew members quickly back to Earth in any emergency.

51

Plans call for the space station to be expanded gradually. A fourth set of solar panels is to be added, permanent-crew quarters will be expanded from four to eight, and a second laboratory will be added. Since the design of Freedom is modular, there is no real limit to its expansion.

Freedom's propulsion assembly will maintain or adjust the orbit of the space station. Its Mobile Servicing System will use an all-purpose robotic arm that can be transported anywhere in space to assemble or repair the station. The special arm and control unit are being supplied by the Canadian Space Agency, while the system itself is being developed at NASA's Johnson Space Center.

Space Station Freedom will become an important biological laboratory. Starting with Spacelab missions in 1985, scientists have been growing protein crystals in microgravity. On Earth, gravity disturbs the growth, making it hard to analyze the structure of these important life molecules. Spacelab produced some protein crystals more perfect than those formed on Earth. On Space Station Freedom such experiments can be carried out over very long periods of time in what is called the Advanced Protein Crystal Growth Facility, or APCGF. These space-crystal studies may hold the key to solving problems of genetics, cancer, and diseases of the human immune system.

Space Psychology

Long-term comfort is highly important to the crew of Space Station Freedom. More than before, astronauts, researchers, and visitors will be far from home, family, and Earth communities. A new kind of permanent space living will take the place of these familiar patterns. Already astronauts can prepare for space life by staying in isolated submarines underwater. But the demands of permanent space living will be much greater.

Psychologists with the Human Factors Office at NASA's Ames Research Center in California are concerned about the effects of such lengthy stays aboard Freedom. To avoid a shut-in feeling they suggest using colors for the crew's living quarters and installing artificial lighting with dimmer switches to simulate day and night.

People sent to live on Space Station Freedom will have to cope well with each other as well as with the rigors of space living. No one can say that any single personality type suits space living best. But the Crew Factors Team at Ames has set up tests to detect psychological weaknesses that might present a problem during stays in space.

There must also be cooperation between the space crew and those working at Mission Control on the ground. Sometimes astronauts feel that they should be more in control because they are the ones actually carrying out the mission. This came up with the crew of Skylab in 1974. The crew thought they had an unworkable schedule and simply went "on strike" for a whole day, until Mission Control agreed to a work-and-rest schedule that was more realistic. In 1985 the Soviets had a different psychological problem. Cosmonaut Vladimir Vasyutin had spent almost two months in space. He began to show signs of stress and became severely depressed. He was returned to

Earth and hospitalized because of his physical or mental condition.

Another consideration is the long-term effect of being away from one's family. An astronaut who leaves a spouse and children behind on Earth will feel very isolated from them. Frequent radio communication can help, but it is hard to keep up a relationship between people separated for some time by distances of space.

Eventually people will spend so long in space that they will fall in love and wish to have families there. No one knows whether the first babies born in space will be on Space Station Freedom, in a more advanced future station, or perhaps even on Mars. But the effects will be profound. The babies will grow in the new environment with different gravity or microgravity. Will they be healthy? Will they develop very differently? And how will the new type of "space family" relate to more traditional families back on Earth? All these questions will have to be answered if humans are to be successful in venturing into space permanently.

Space Suits and Simulators

On Earth we live at the bottom of an ocean of air. About 20 percent of this is the oxygen that sustains life as we know it. This atmosphere presses against our bodies at around 14.7 pounds per square inch at sea level. At 18,000 feet above sea level the pressure drops to about half that. Airplanes using pressurized cabins routinely carry people up to twice that high.

Above 40,000 feet the air is so thin that pressure oxygen masks are not sufficient even in an emergency. And above 63,000 feet, blood will boil if a human is exposed to outer space.

During the Mercury missions a single astronaut orbited the earth in a small, pressurized capsule. The space suit was an improved version of the one used by the Navy for high-altitude jet airplanes. The inner layer was made of a specially coated nylon fabric, and the outer layer was of aluminized nylon. The pressurized Mercury suit felt constricting because the fabric was folded inward at the body joints. During orbital flights the suit was left unpressurized. It was worn as a backup in case of an emergency loss of capsule pressure.

The suit for the Gemini missions was based on an Air Force design and allowed for greater mobility. The inner layer, called the pressure bladder, was made of specially coated nylon filled with gas. It was shaped to fit the astronaut who wore the suit. An outer restraint layer was woven from Dacron and Teflon cords to form a net. This layer kept the inner one from over-expanding.

When Apollo missions took astronauts to the moon, space suits were further strengthened. Because of the risk of tears and punctures or bombardment by tiny meteorites, an outer protective layer was added. Mobility was improved by using rubber joints that expanded like bellows at the shoulders, elbows, hips, and knees. Beginning with *Apollo 15*, the suits also folded at the waist so astronauts could sit and drive the lunar rovers.

The side of a space suit facing the sun can heat to as much

as 250 degrees F. Therefore, an insulation layer and a cooling network were necessary. The innermost layer of the Apollo suit, the liquid cooling garment, contained tiny tubes sewed into the fabric. Cool water was pumped through the tubes to carry excess heat to a backpack, which released the heat into space. The next layer was of lightweight nylon. Over this came the pressure bladder and restraint layers. Next came a layer of lightweight thermal insulation. This was covered by a layer of Mylar and lastly by a protective cloth of glass fibers and Teflon.

The helmets for Apollo missions were attached to the suit by a seal. The Apollo helmet was large enough for the astronaut's head to freely turn inside it instead of the helmet's turning with the head. For use on the moon's surface, an outer visor was added to the helmet to shield the astronaut from the sun's ultraviolet radiation and to keep the helmet from getting too cool or hot. The final parts of the lunar space suit were flexible gloves and heavy-duty boots for walking over the rocky surface.

Clothing for space shuttle flights is much more varied. Through ascent and reentry stages crew members wear partially pressurized suits and a parachute harness and emergency pack. The suit includes a helmet, a communications unit, and gloves and boots. If the orbiter loses cabin pressure, the suit's bladder layer will inflate.

Inside the space shuttle, crew members work in short-sleeved shirts, knit shirts, flight suits or trousers, or lined jackets. Underwear, sleepwear, and even slippers are part of the regular garb. It feels like ordinary clothing except that every-

Astronaut Kenneth Reightler puts on the partially pressurized garment worn for shuttle missions during launch and atmospheric reentry.

thing is made flame retardant in case of fire. Jackets close easily with zippers, and large outside pockets hold writing tools, Swiss Army work knives, sunglasses, and other items.

On some shuttle flights the cargo bay holds a satellite or experimental device to be placed into orbit. Then an astronaut uses the extravehicular mobility unit, or EMU, space suit. The complete EMU includes the suit itself, the primary life-support system (PLSS), a display and control module to monitor breathing, communications, and other functions, and any extra systems necessary for a spacewalk.

To suit up, the astronaut enters the airlock module of the space shuttle orbiter. The first part of the EMU to go on is a

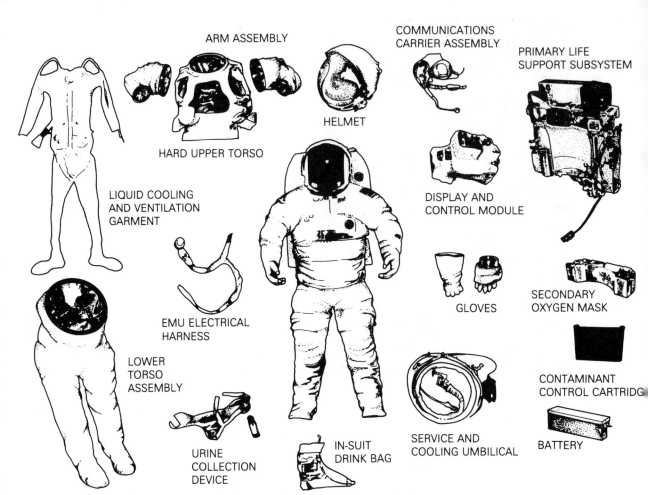

ARM ASSEMBLY

COMMUNICATIONS
CARRIER ASSEMBLY

PRIMARY LIFE
SUPPORT SUBSYSTEM

HELMET

HARD UPPER TORSO

LIQUID COOLING
AND VENTILATION
GARMENT

DISPLAY AND
CONTROL MODULE

EMU ELECTRICAL
HARNESS

GLOVES

SECONDARY
OXYGEN MASK

LOWER
TORSO
ASSEMBLY

CONTAMINANT
CONTROL CARTRIDG

URINE
COLLECTION
DEVICE

IN-SUIT
DRINK BAG

SERVICE AND
COOLING UMBILICAL

BATTERY

Space shuttle EMU space suit components

unit to collect urine, which will be transferred later to the
orbiter's waste management system. Next is a cooling garment
that zips closed from the front. Then comes a bag full of drinking
water. Following this is a communications assembly with head-
phones, microphones, and medical monitors.

The astronaut first puts on the lower torso assembly. Then

he or she drifts up through zero G into the upper torso section that is fastened to the wall of the airlock. This is a hard fiberglass shell that contains the primary life-support system and the display and control module. Gloves are added, and finally the helmet and visor. The completed suit has joints with roller bearings, so the astronaut can bend and twist fairly easily. In addition to the pressure bladder and restraint layers, there is also an outside antiabrasion layer that resists tears and punctures. The whole EMU suit weighs up to 107 pounds. Of course in zero G the suit has no weight. It is simply a "floating" mass covering the astronaut, ready to be maneuvered from place to place.

Before moving out into space, the astronaut secures any tools to a mini work station that is part of the suit. Helmet lights are turned on because, during Earth orbit, every 45-minute period of sunlight is followed by a 45-minute period of darkness.

When Ed White made the first U.S. excursion into space from the capsule of *Gemini 4*, he was attached to the capsule with a tether containing his oxygen lifeline. The Apollo moon astronauts wore life-support units on their backs.

On the moon 180 pounds of suit and equipment felt like only about 30 pounds to the astronauts because of the moon's low gravity. The lunar astronauts could jump in a kind of slow motion and walk reasonably well on the moon's surface. Nevertheless they were bound by gravity to a planetary body. During shuttle EVAs the astronauts operate independently of gravity in space.

The device that gives the shuttle astronauts total space mobility is the manned maneuvering unit (MMU). The MMU has sophisticated controls. An electrical harness inside the suit connects the chest display and control module to an extravehicular communicator mounted at the upper back of the suit. Using UHF channels, the astronaut can broadcast to and receive signals from the orbiter. The built-in medical monitor sends heart EKG signals to the orbiter, which in turn relays them to flight surgeons at ground Mission Control.

The primary life-support system itself is a backpack mounted permanently to the suit's upper torso. It is adjusted with the chest control. The PLSS supplies oxygen for breathing and removes carbon dioxide. It regulates gas temperatures and cools the water circulating through the ventilation garment. The PLSS also removes odors from the circulating gases.

Free of the orbiter, the astronaut floats in a vacuum. There is nothing to push off from or to "swim" in. In this environment the manned maneuvering unit must be used. It is attached to the PLSS, and arms with built-in hand controls extend on either side like the arms of a chair. There are two control systems; should one fail, the other can get the astronaut back to the orbiter.

The MMU works like a small rocket. Pressurized nitrogen gas is released into space in short bursts. The gas particles released in one direction push the MMU and astronaut in the opposite direction. Using the hand controls to change the angle of released nitrogen, the astronaut can rotate, tumble, or drift

Kathryn Sullivan, the first U.S. woman to perform an untethered space EVA, tests a Manned Maneuvering Unit as she floats in the Johnson Space Center's underwater training facility.

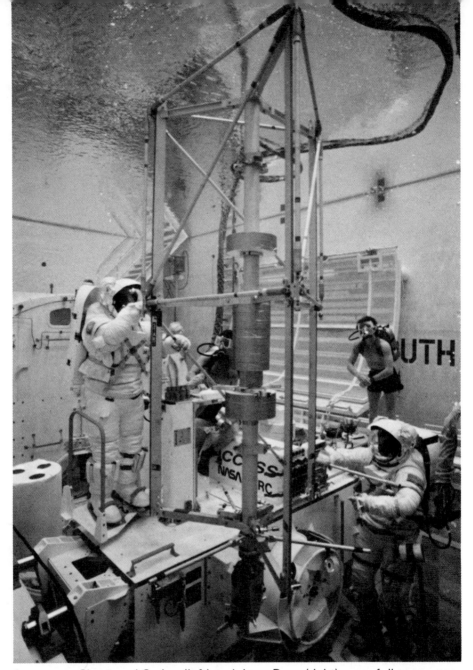

Astronauts Sherwood Spring (left) and Jerry Ross (right) wear full space gear underwater while doing a simulated space construction in the Weightless Environment Training Facility at Johnson Space Center.

in any direction. The astronaut is a self-contained spacecraft, moving and living in the void of outer space.

Bruce McCandless was the first astronaut to use the MMU outside the shuttle in February 1984. The MMU then became standard for space shuttle EVAs.

Astronauts must train in the suits they will use in space. And they must also train in simulators that mimic weightlessness, the thrust of rocket lift-off, and other conditions they will encounter. These simulator trainers are located at various NASA facilities around the United States. One such trainer is the deepwater swimming pool called the Neutral Buoyancy Simulator (NBS), at the Marshall Space Flight Center in California. Water is the Earth environment closest to that of gravity-free space, and at the proper depth an astronaut in full gear will hang suspended in the NBS as he or she would in the microgravity of outer space. In this buoyant environment astronauts are trained and operations that will be carried out in space are tested.

When Skylab was launched in 1973, its sunshield was damaged and its solar panels failed to open. Simulated repairs were tried underwater in the NBS tank. At exactly the same time Skylab was being repaired in space, engineers at Marshall were in the tank ready to give advice step by step.

An even more impressive-looking setup at Marshall is the Teleoperator and Robotics Evaluation Facility. This fills more than 11,000 square feet of space. Huge robotic arms move at the push of a button or the twist of a hand control. Trainees

Space shuttle simulators at Johnson Space Center. The one in the foreground has a remote manipulator arm. Controlled from the flight deck console at the left, it maneuvers a helium-filled "satellite" from the shuttle cargo bay.

learn to estimate direction, distance, and angle of the remote units in order to perform difficult tasks.

Another simulator facility is at the Johnson Space Center (JSC) in Houston, Texas. JSC has simulators that reproduce shuttle and Spacelab modules for crew training, as well as its own underwater tank, called the Weightless Environment Training Facility, or WET-F. There researchers are developing models of two space suits for use aboard Space Station Freedom, the AX-5, and the Mark III.

The test design of an advanced space helmet that projects computer images on a transparent visor.

Sue Schentrup wears a prototype of the high-pressure Mark 3 space suit, which is planned for EVAs at short notice aboard Space Station Freedom.

The experience of training in simulators has even been extended to youngsters and adults interested in space education. The unusual program is located at the U.S. Space and Rocket Center in Huntsville, Alabama. "Space Camp" and "Space Academy" programs are available for everyone from fourth graders to adults. There is firsthand experience for young people who want to learn about space-age careers. Students stay at the facility for several days and are introduced to a wide variety of space-training equipment. There is even a special five-day program for teachers who want to include space study in their own classrooms.

Astronauts train in a variety of different simulators to condition themselves for space activities. The microgravity trainer, part seat and part harness, is adjustable to provide an exact degree of lift when pushing off against Earth's gravity. For instance, when operating as a "moonwalk trainer," it makes the astronaut feel as if gravity is only one sixth that on earth. Every jump is huge.

The 1-G trainer is a seat with hand controls to enable the astronaut to maneuver in any direction—sideways or upside down—against normal gravity. This is like the action of the MMU in outer space. The Multi-Axis Trainer goes a step further. This large device of interlocking rings turns its occupant wildly to simulate a spacecraft tumbling out of control. In an EVA trainer, astronauts are suspended from cables and booms to simulate doing a repair outside a space capsule. They also train in a centrifuge. This can spin the occupant to increase

A Space Camp student moves cubes with a robotic arm assembly.

The Multi-Axis Trainer at the U.S. Space and Rocket Center in Huntsville, Alabama

gravity to up to three Gs, or three times Earth gravity—simulating the thrust of lift-off.

All these simulators are useful in giving astronauts the experience of zero G and the feel of movements and controls before they actually encounter them in space.

Such training was put to special use in May of 1992, when astronauts Richard Hieb, Thomas Akers, and Pierre Thout performed the first three-person EVA outside NASA's newest space shuttle, the *Endeavor.* Part of *Endeavor*'s mission was to rescue

Mission Specialists Richard Hieb, Thomas Akers, and Pierre Thout on the manipulator arm at right steady Intelsat VI outside space shuttle *Endeavor.* During this first three-person EVA, the communications satellite was rescued and boosted into proper Earth orbit.

a 4.5-ton Intelsat communications satellite that had fallen into a low orbit.

As Mission Specialist Thout stood on the end of the remote manipulator arm, the team of three held and steadied the huge Intelsat for one and a half hours until the retrieving equipment was securely fastened. After a small booster rocket was attached, the satellite was successfully released toward a higher geosynchronous orbit to serve worldwide communications links.

3

TO MARS AND BEYOND

One goal of the Directive on National Space Policy issued by President Bush was "to expand human presence and activity beyond earth orbit into the solar system." Anticipating this goal, the National Commission on Space had already recommended a clear U.S. plan in 1986: "To lead the exploration and development of the space frontier, advancing science, technology, and enterprise, and building institutions and systems that make accessible vast new resources and support human settlements beyond Earth orbit, from the highlands of the moon to the plains of Mars."

The same year NASA asked astronaut Sally Ride, the first U.S. woman into space, to guide a task force to look into planned space exploration. The result was the Ride Report, called "Leadership and America's Future in Space."

There were four parts: Mission to Planet Earth; Exploration of the Solar System; Outpost on the Moon; and Humans to Mars.

The report suggested that exploration could take two paths. First we could place a permanent outpost on the moon. From the moon we could then launch interplanetary flights to Mars. Or missions could be launched to a moon of Mars from Earth orbit. Then, using this moon as an outpost, missions to Mars could be made.

Certainly observatories and outposts on the moon would be valuable. However, missions to Mars and its moons might be easier from space platforms already orbiting Earth.

Two Ways to Mars

According to the Ride Report, missions to Mars could follow two different plans. Under the first plan exploration of outer space begins with a return to the moon. The timetable might be arranged like this: A series of crewed flights would leave for the moon around the year 2004. Chemically propelled vehicles would be used for these flights. Once on the moon, astronauts would travel over the surface with a nuclear-powered rover. Over a period of several years a permanent base would be constructed. Part would be aboveground and part underground for protection. It would be staffed with rotating crews from Earth.

During this time, we would be gaining experience living on a remote planetlike body. Although Earth is only a journey of

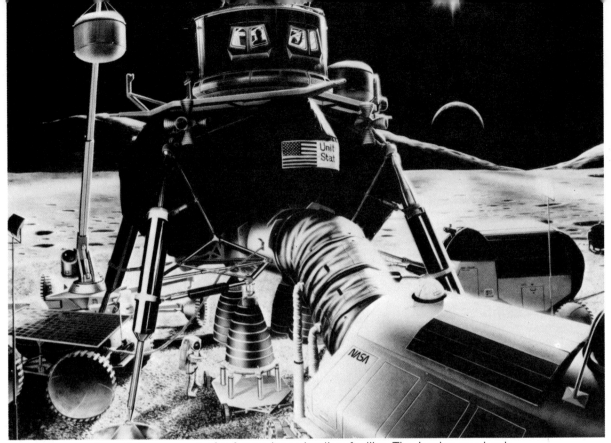

An artist's concept of a future lunar landing facility. The lander on shock-absorbing legs has just arrived. The pressurized vehicle in the foreground will take the crew to the moon base, as fueling and engine technicians work on the lander.

a few days away, the astronauts would live off the resources of the moon itself. Plants for food would be grown in a pressurized greenhouse. A facility would be set up to extract oxygen from the lunar soil. Growing plants would use up carbon dioxide and release additional oxygen to help provide a permanent enclosed environment. Some of the oxygen drawn from the soil would also be compressed into the liquid oxygen needed for rocket fuel.

Around the year 2010, at a time when the two planets are close together, preparations for a flight to Mars would be complete. First a robotic electric-powered cargo shuttle would be launched from Earth, carrying scientific equipment and vehicles to Mars. The cargo shuttle would arrive at Phobos, one of the two small moons circling Mars. As it approached Mars, the shuttle would automatically place communications satellites into Mars orbit. It would also deliver to Phobos a technical system for producing rocket fuel once humans arrive.

At the next close encounter between Earth and Mars, a second electric vehicle would be launched to our own moon

A proposed plant separates oxygen from water derived from basalt rocks in a moon crater.

carrying an empty crew transport ship. The crew transport would automatically go into lunar orbit to await the arrival of a human crew. Meanwhile the electric vehicle would return to Earth. The actual Mars flight crew would then journey from Earth to dock with the orbiting transport ship. After it is fueled with liquid oxygen from the moon, the crew would begin its eight-month journey to Mars.

The journey must be planned for a time when Earth and Mars are both on the same side of the sun, a situation that happens only once every twenty-six months. This way, if the crew encounters any trouble, it could return to Earth immediately or stay on Mars for up to sixty days. If the decision to return is made within this period, the trip back would still take only about eight months.

Beyond the sixty-day limit the crew would have to live on Mars for an extended time. It would not be practical to attempt to return to Earth until the next close encounter of Earth and Mars a little over two years later. The distance would be too great, and too much time and fuel would be required.

The other plan for travel to Mars is to go directly from Earth to Phobos. This is simpler than using our moon as a way station. As in the first plan, equipment would be transported to Phobos, followed closely by a manned crew.

There are several reasons for choosing Phobos as a landing site. Phobos is more like an artificial satellite than a moon, with a low orbit. This orbit makes it a convenient base. Phobos is only about seventeen miles long and five miles wide—the size

A human mission to Mars' tiny moon, Phobos. Astronauts use personal spacecraft tethered to anchors on the surface. Mars looms in the background, with the orbiting spaceship circling it.

of a small island. It is so tiny, it has almost no gravity. An astronaut would seem to weigh about three ounces, and everything would have to be anchored to the surface to keep it in place. Less fuel, and therefore less weight, would be required to launch a mission first to Phobos rather than to Mars.

Once a crew had settled on Phobos, missions to Mars would be as easy as relanding a shuttle from Earth orbit. Since Mars has an atmosphere, a landing craft could deploy a saucer-shaped "aerobrake" to help slow descent to the surface. Little fuel would be required, though, since the Martian air is very thin and the pull of gravity only about one third that of Earth. Returning a crew to Earth after either a few months or a longer two-year stay would be done from Phobos rather than from Mars, again saving weight and fuel for the homeward journey.

Plans are not yet set. Proposals that followed the Ride Report, including the Augustine and Stafford Reports, aim for travel directly to Mars. Scientists will refine plans until we actually launch humans to Mars.

Planetary Environment

Mars is the fourth planet out from the sun, one of Earth's neighbors in space. It is only one half Earth's diameter and is less dense, so it has a lighter gravitational pull. If you weigh 100 pounds on Earth, you would weigh about thirty-eight pounds on Mars. A day on Mars is almost exactly the same as an Earth day, since Mars rotates once every 24 hours and 37 minutes. Like Earth, Mars is tipped on its axis, so there are seasonal changes. However, a year is nearly twice as long, since Mars takes 687 days to go around the sun.

When Mars was seen through early telescopes, it seemed to have a network of lines, or "canals." Close observations sent by NASA's Mariner flyby in 1965 and Viking landers in 1976 showed instead meandering valleys and deep canyons. These look like channels and gorges on Earth, except that on Mars none of these ditches holds any water. Evidently, very long ago, Mars had lakes and rivers that later dried up as surface conditions changed.

Mountains on Mars are higher than any on Earth. For example, the peak of Earth's Mount Everest reaches over 29,000 feet. Olympus Mons, Mars' highest volcanic mountain, rises around 90,000 feet. So far this is the highest one known on any

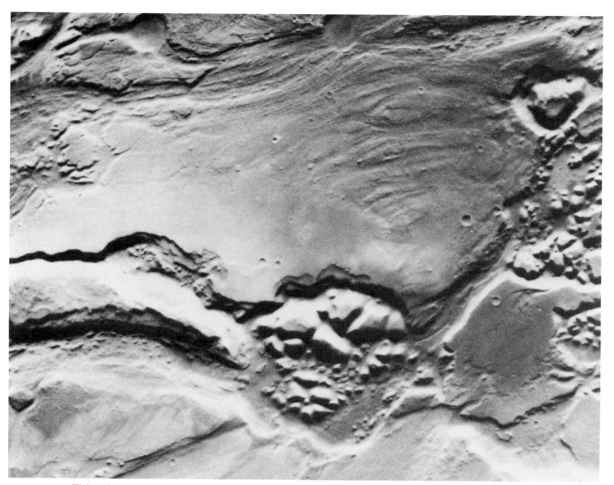

This photo of Mars from the Viking orbiter shows a complex channel system with layers of sediment. Many Martian gorges resemble dried riverbeds and lake beds once formed by surface water.

of the planets in our solar system. Olympus Mons rests on top of the Tharsis Plain, a huge, raised area as big as the United States. And Mars' deepest canyon, found near its equator, stretches 2,800 miles—about the distance from New York to San Francisco.

One reason for these dramatic surface features is that the

crust of Mars does not seem to shift. When Earth's crust drifts, a volcano will gradually shift away from its position over the hot inner region that formed it. But on Mars a volcano stays in place and continues to build.

Mars has riverbeds and what seem to be dried-up lakes. Ancient meteorite craters now lie on top of some of them, suggesting that as far back as 3.8 billion years ago conditions on Mars were different than they are today. Then Mars must have had a heavy carbon dioxide atmosphere, and its surface was at least warm enough for rainfall and running water and lakes. Over the eons much of the atmosphere was lost, the planet cooled, and the surface water disappeared.

Today Mars still has a carbon dioxide atmosphere. But it is thin—about the density of Earth's atmosphere at twenty miles above the surface. On a hot summer day on Mars, at the equator, the temperature might go up to a pleasant 60° F. But the temperature at night at the same place could be as cold as $-125°F$. The overall average temperature of Mars is a chilling 76 degrees Fahrenheit below zero.

In order for a planet to be habitable for Earth settlers, there must be a balance of atmospheric factors, chiefly carbon dioxide, oxygen, and water vapor. When a planetary atmosphere is rich in carbon dioxide and water vapor, light from the sun is allowed to reach the surface. At the same time those gases block heat from escaping back into space from the warmed surface. When temperatures are held above freezing, water vapor can condense as rain. Oceans, lakes, and running rivers form. Water evaporates from the water surface and collects again in the atmosphere. A climate and water cycle like ours on Earth can then perpetuate itself.

On Earth, carbon dioxide gas dissolves in rain, and the rainwater reacts chemically with surface rocks. The carbon and oxygen molecules are carried into streams, rivers, and oceans. There the molecules become components of seashells that later form layers on the bottoms of the seas. As continents slowly drift, this sediment finds its way to hot, inner regions of the earth. Once again carbon dioxide is released into the atmosphere in the gases of erupting volcanoes. Though this cycle may take 500,000 years, it is important in regulating Earth's environment.

Here's how it works: Suppose Earth's temperature fell and seas began to freeze. Less water would evaporate and less rain would fall, so less dissolved carbon dioxide would be brought to surface waters. However, volcanoes would still release carbon dioxide, so more would collect in the atmosphere. This in turn would form a blanket around Earth allowing less heat to escape. The planet would get warmer, ice would melt, and more carbon dioxide would then be dissolved in falling rain. Earth's temperature has been regulated in this way for millions of years.

This cycle is also affected by the presence of life. On Earth, plants absorb carbon dioxide and release oxygen. Animals in turn absorb oxygen and release carbon dioxide. So even though a planet may be habitable without life, the presence of life adds another cycle to the delicate balance.

Some scientists believe Earth and its nearest neighbors, Mars and Venus, were once more alike. They had similar surface minerals and similar gases in their atmospheres, including carbon dioxide and water vapor. These atmospheres changed on Venus and Mars, however, because their planetary cycles could not remain stable.

On Venus, the next planet closer to the sun than Earth, extra sunlight may have broken up water vapor in the atmosphere, allowing its hydrogen to escape as a gas. The planet may have become a "greenhouse" too hot to hold water on the surface. Without large amounts of water vapor, the planet became too hot to sustain life.

Mars is the next planet from the sun beyond Earth. Because of its smaller size, Mars had less internal heat when it formed. As surface features show, water was once present there for a very long time. The same rain, sediment, and volcanic cycle would have existed on Mars as on Earth. Possibly because Mars' crust does not shift, there was less chance for carbon dioxide to be released from seashell-like material that became heated underground. At any rate something in the cycle of carbon dioxide and water vapor broke down, and Mars cooled. Still, Mars probably has carbon dioxide trapped in buried rocks.

Today there is almost no water vapor in Mars' atmosphere. Much of it is trapped in the planet's south polar ice cap and probably held as permafrost beneath the surface. If sizeable amounts of trapped carbon dioxide and water vapor were released, a new cycle could be set into action that would warm the climate of Mars once again.

Some of the deep canyons of Mars probably formed as the crust cracked, and later these filled with groundwater. Other channels may have eroded in great floods that occurred when ice dams melted and released huge amounts of trapped underground water. Evidence suggests that a warmer and heavier carbon dioxide atmosphere covered Mars for hundreds of millions of years in its early development, then disappeared.

Primitive Life

Mars may well have been home to primitive life during its wet period. One kind of primitive life that still exists on Earth is the stromatolites. These microscopic organisms are found in shallow water and form large, spongy mats containing both living organisms and those that have died or become fossilized. As lands and seas have changed over millions of years, fossil layers of stromatolites have become deeply buried. These primitive organisms grew in the presence of sunlight and carbon dioxide, which was also abundant in Mars' early atmosphere.

Photos of Mars from Viking missions show layers of sediment in the lakelike depressions. They resemble deposits formed in standing water on Earth. Such layers can be seen in the floors of many of the canyons around what is called the Valles Marineris, a system of channels surrounding the raised Tharsis Plain of Mars.

On Earth, layers of both living and fossilized stromatolites have been found under ice-covered lakes in Antarctica. These lakes are found in Antarctica's "dry valleys"—the parts of the south polar continent that are not covered by glacial land ice. Rocky surfaces are exposed in the dry valleys. Conditions and temperatures there are much like those on Mars today. The rocky valleys contain riverbeds as well as lakes. Even though summertime temperatures are above freezing for only a few days, enough glacial ice melts into the valleys to cut river channels that feed into the ice-covered lakes. Thus even in a region of Earth averaging $-4°$ F through the year, running water can slowly form surface features. The same could have happened on Mars.

In Antarctica the dry valley lakes are frozen to an average depth of about fifteen feet. Under this the temperature of the water stays just above freezing. The melting water running into the lakes brings dissolved gases from the atmosphere. Thus the lake waters contain much greater amounts of oxygen, carbon

Proposed training base in the dry valleys of southern Victoria Land, Antarctica. The weather and terrain resemble those on Mars, where dry depressions may once have held ice-covered lakes.

dioxide, and nitrogen than the air above. In these conditions enough sunlight penetrates the ice layer for microscopic plant life to thrive in underwater mats that drift upward from the lake bed.

It is likely that primitive microorganisms similar to these developed on Mars during the millions of years when it had a thick atmosphere and surface water and ice. And it is even possible that this life still exists in scattered pockets of liquid water trapped in various places on the planet.

Mars Probes

During the 1990s, several important planetary probes are going to Mars and beyond. The Mars Observer spacecraft was launched in September of 1992. It is the first U.S. orbiter scheduled to go there since Viking in 1976. Observer's two-year mission will actually begin in December of 1993. The orbiting satellite will take photographs, analyze Mars' gravitational and magnetic fields, and map the mineral composition of the surface. It will also store computerized information on Martian seasons, dust storms, and weather patterns.

Meanwhile the former Soviet Union, now the Commonwealth of Independent States (CIS), plans a "Mars 1994" mission to place a satellite into orbit around Mars early in 1996. This orbiter will carry a special balloon instrument assembly built by France. The balloon will descend through Mars' atmosphere to the surface. It will remain there at night, but daylight heat will cause the balloon to expand and rise again

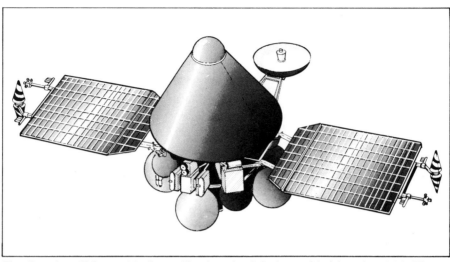

The Russian "Mars 1994" satellite is scheduled to orbit Mars in 1996. There it will release a balloon probe built by French engineers.

within the atmosphere. The daily ascents and descents will permit cameras and instruments to relay valuable information to the CIS orbiter. NASA's Mars Observer will also monitor the balloon information. In a cooperative venture, both the CIS and U.S. satellites will broadcast information to Earth. The CIS plans further launches in 1996, in 1998, and then in the year 2001. These will include orbiters, surface rovers, weather stations, and balloons that will drag the Martian surface for samples.

Up to twelve nations are joining in missions planned by the European Space Agency, along with the Japanese. United States robot launches to Mars are scheduled for 1998, 2001, 2003, 2005, 2007, 2009, and 2014. And a major goal for the

United States and NASA is a human landing on Mars sometime between the years 2014 and 2018.

Living on Mars

Designing a space suit for the thin Martian air is easier than making one for outer space. In the vacuum of space the side of a space suit facing the sun becomes extremely hot while the other side loses heat to the utter cold of outer space. However, on Mars the atmosphere makes heat absorption and loss much more even. The astronaut's perspiration could carry excess heat through the suit to the cold outside air. In addition it may be possible to use an oxygen breather that is similar to scuba gear. Oxygen would pass once through the system and then be released into the atmosphere. These advantages mean that suits for Martian astronauts can be much lighter and more flexible than those needed in outer space.

A new idea has been proposed for moving people quickly over Mars' deserts and gulleys. It was developed by engineers at Martin Marietta Corporation and is called NIMF, which stands for Nuclear Rocket Using Indigenous Martian Fuel. The idea is a rocket that hops from place to place on the surface of the planet. Whenever the "hopper" lands, scientists will spend several weeks exploring the surface. Meanwhile the hopper refuels by drawing carbon dioxide from the atmosphere, compressing it to a liquid, and storing it in tanks until it is used. The fuel will be heated by nuclear power and used to propel the hopper to the next location. The process is both simple and inexpensive.

Rovers driven on Earth's moon used electrical power from batteries or solar cells. On Mars, where reliable power is needed for longer distances, chemical engines would be more useful. Such an engine could burn carbon dioxide, hydrogen, or methane. Because Mars' atmosphere is so thin, the engine would have to work like the engine in a high-altitude plane on

An artist's view of a robotic Mars rover gathering data and soil samples

Earth: An extra supply of oxygen would combine with the fuels to help ignite them. Nuclear or solar devices would supply power to trigger the gas. The engine would be partly cooled just by the cold temperatures on Mars.

Water is essential to supporting human life on Mars. There are several sources on the planet. The atmosphere holds some as water vapor, larger amounts are probably buried in permafrost layers, and water ice is frozen in the polar caps.

However, a practical way to get water on Mars is to "farm" it. Just like a farm on Earth, a flat area would be cleared of boulders and other debris. Since the grainy Martian soil holds a limited amount of absorbed water drawn from the atmosphere, a farmer could "harvest" it. A special tractor with both a water-vapor collection vacuum and a microwave heater is needed. The microwave device is aimed at the soil and heats it. This drives off water vapor. A vacuum system then sucks in the water vapor, and it is condensed on cooling fins like the moist air in an air conditioner. The farmer simply drives the water tractor up and down the soil plot. After a time a field that had been "water harvested" would reabsorb some of the sparse moisture from the atmosphere and could be farmed again. The water "crop" would slowly but constantly renew itself.

Terraforming

Because Mars once had a planetary cycle similar to that of Earth, there are two exciting possibilities. One is that some form of life may have developed there in earlier times. The other is that the atmosphere might be changed back to one that will support human life. This process is called terraforming. "Terra" means Earth, and so the word means making an environment like that of Earth.

Mars has all the resources needed for this to happen. Using these, it is possible to artificially alter the atmosphere, temperature, and surface to create a place where people could walk without space suits, breathe the air, and go about life as we do on our home planet.

The change can be made in a series of ingenious steps. The technology for such a task is available. Remarkably, it could possibly be done in less than two hundred years. Thus, within a few generations a long evolutionary process could be gone through in a mere instant of cosmic time.

Suppose that Mars has already been explored by Earth travelers and that by around the year 2030 there are permanent bases. These would be producing their own food, oxygen, water, fuel, and other essentials. The emphasis of the technology could then be turned to warming the planet.

The first step would be to create a "greenhouse" effect in the atmosphere. One way is to have chemical factories pump fluorocarbons into the air. These are the gases in refrigerants and other sources that we are trying to keep out of Earth's atmosphere so it does not get too hot. Instead, on Mars these gases would gather in the atmosphere and purposely prevent surface heat from escaping.

The second step is to make the polar ice darker in color so

An early Mars colony with facilities for altering atmospheric gases and for mining or "farming" water, and greenhouses for growing food plants

that it reflects less heat and becomes warmer. Black powder could be spread over the poles, or microorganisms could be deposited that would multiply and cover the ice with a film. The ice would eventually look something like a giant asphalt parking lot that absorbs more winter heat than it reflects.

To speed up the thaw of polar ice, mirrors could be launched into polar orbit. These would be angled to reflect sunlight onto the polar caps as they pass overhead, also causing the ice to melt.

As temperatures rise, carbon dioxide and water vapor would be released from the ice into the atmosphere. At the same time the warming of rocks on the surface would release trapped carbon dioxide, nitrogen, and water vapor.

Next a gas similar to the ozone found high in Earth's atmosphere would be pumped into Mars' atmosphere. Each ozone molecule contains three bonded oxygen atoms. Ozone shades the planet from damaging ultraviolet rays of the sun. All these steps to create a warmer protective atmosphere on Mars might be accomplished by about the year 2080.

By this time enough factors would be at work for Mars to continue to warm itself. Between the years 2080 and 2115 the surface temperature would rise from an average 40° below zero to an average of around 5° F above. This is still not very warm, but surface water would gather in some places, and tundra vegetation could be planted to grow as it does on Earth near the Arctic Circle. Such vegetation could survive on the increasing carbon dioxide in the Martian atmosphere. Clouds would form, and the color of the sky would have changed gradually from pink to blue. Atmospheric pressure would have increased to around half that of Earth. It would be like living on the mountains of Earth, and pressurized space suits would no longer be needed. Instead, oxygen tanks and rebreathing masks could be used.

During this phase the Mars tundra plants would be releasing

some oxygen into the air. Much more would be generated by taking advantage of a characteristic of Martian soil: Mars has a coating of iron oxide, which is a combination of iron and oxygen. There is so much of this that the planet looks reddish from a distance. Heating the plentiful iron oxide would release large quantities of oxygen into the atmosphere.

As the amount of oxygen increases, the air pressure would also continue to increase. In the period between 2115 and around 2130 the pressure would rise to about double that on Earth. Since Mars is half again as far from the sun as Earth, this thicker atmosphere is needed to hold the required heat. This extra pressure is still in a comfortable range for humans.

Once these changes were underway, the tundralike vegetation would spread over more of Mars' surface. Evergreens like those high on Earth's mountains could begin to be grown there. The temperature would rise from about 5° F above zero to an average of 32° F above zero, the melting temperature of water ice.

Between 2130 and about 2150, the temperature of Mars would reach an average of around 40° F. Much of the permafrost layer beneath the soil would have melted, along with most of the water at the poles. The water vapor released into the atmosphere would fall as rain. Running water would fill many of Mars' gorges and canyons. Its lake beds would be full of carbonated water from the carbon dioxide in the atmosphere. New streams would erode the surface. The cycle of evaporation and rainfall would work as it does on Earth. Many kinds of crops could be grown. Oxygen in the atmosphere would have increased dramatically, but portable breathers would still be used.

From 2150 to perhaps 2170, oxygen would still be added artificially to the atmosphere. The process would speed up as plant life spread over the surface, absorbing carbon dioxide and releasing oxygen. When the oxygen level reaches around two thirds that in Earth's atmosphere, human and animal life would finally be able to breathe freely.

By this date new generations of people would have been born on Mars and grown up there. These people would be more adapted to living on Mars than to living on Earth. Their lungs and rib cages would probably be larger than those of earthlings. Because of Mars' lighter gravity, their bones would likely be less dense and more porous. Arms and legs might be longer than those of humans living on Earth.

These new generations of Martians might feel as uncomfortable visiting Earth as some earlier generations of Earth dwellers will have felt when first attempting to live on Mars. These "men from Mars" would be descended from us, but would be true "Martians" nonetheless. Mars would no longer be just a large colony of explorers from Earth but a planetary home to its own people.

Future Travel

One important step toward better space travel will be the space airplane. The U.S. space shuttle can drop from space orbit, resist the heat of atmospheric reentry, and then land like a high-speed glider. But it must be lifted into orbit by a rocket whose sections are retrieved after an ocean splashdown. This is a wasteful way to get a small capsule into orbit. It is better to have an airplane that is capable of reaching the speed for Earth orbit, and that can later land like the space shuttle.

Since the 1960s the possibility of such a plane has been studied. One U.S. project, called Dyna-Soar, was proposed by the Air Force but never carried out. Other proposals have been made by designers from various countries. The European Space Agency had planned development of a space plane called Hermes during the 1990s. However, the plan has been temporarily cancelled.

Meanwhile, a step in this direction was made by the Russians. Although there has been no official announcement, an Australian airplane crossing the Indian Ocean photographed a model space plane being rescued from the water after a test flight. It is expected that in the future this plane, managed by CIS, will still be launched by a small rocket. But the plane will be tinier and will have more flight capabilities than a space shuttle. It might be used for space repairs and rescues, or to transport people from one space module to another. It is expected to land on any ordinary runway.

Scientists agree that travel to Mars or beyond will depend on nuclear power. Chemical rockets are fine for boosting astronauts to the moon or for launching satellites on journeys to our outer planets. The moon is only a few days away, and time is not an issue with planetary probes. But getting humans to Mars can take as long as eight or nine months, and round trips would take double that time. Humans on such a journey would spend most of their time in a permanently traveling space module. In addition, extended excursions through outer space subject the craft and its passengers to radiation from solar storms and other sources.

The chemical rockets of today are near their limits of power. To go farther and faster, nuclear rockets will probably be needed. Scientists describe two basic kinds, nuclear-electric and nuclear-thermal. In a nuclear-electric system a reactor produces heat. This is converted to electricity to run the propulsion unit: For example, gas ions passing between two charged plates are ejected as a propellant.

A nuclear-electric system might move an uncrewed cargo vessel to Mars. But much greater speed is possible with a nuclear-thermal system. This system uses a nuclear reactor and a propellant gas such as hydrogen. The reactor heats the hydrogen, and this gas then expands through a rocket nozzle to develop thrust. A solid-core reactor like those in power plants around the world could double the power of chemical rockets.

A group called the Innovative Nuclear Space Power Institute at the University of Florida in Gainesville is working on a third alternative: a gaseous core reactor, which uses a radioactive gas instead of solid material. Such a reactor has not yet been completed, but it may be able to generate as much as five times the power of a nuclear-thermal reactor.

Whatever the type of nuclear propulsion, it will be used as the last stage of launch into space from Earth orbit. In this way, any danger from a damaged nuclear-propulsion system will be minimal.

Concept for a nuclear-thermal rocket by Boeing engineers. Planned as a human space transport, the craft is shown approaching Mars.

To the Stars

The closest star to the sun is Alpha Centauri, about four light-years away. Light travels at about 186,000 miles per second; a light-year is the distance light travels in a year—about 5.9 trillion miles. Our sun is only 8.3 light *seconds* away—some 93 million miles. Even if a nuclear-powered spacecraft could somehow approach the speed of light, it would still take at least four years to reach any planets circling Alpha Centauri. And this is only the closest star. What about others many times more distant?

The chief limitation to distant-space travel seems to be time. However, time can be considered a dimension like length and depth. According to Einstein's theory of relativity, measurements of time are relative. For example, Earth is like a space station traveling around our sun at about 66,600 miles per hour, or 18.5 miles per second. Light travels over 10,000 times faster. But suppose a spaceship can accelerate until it reaches nearly the speed of light. According to relativity, to those on the spacecraft, time would seem to pass as it does on Earth. But to those observing the spacecraft from Earth, time in the spacecraft would seem to have slowed down. A twin brother traveling out from Earth and back at such a speed could find that his sibling had aged much more than he had.

Scientific theory says that the speed of light is a limit that cannot be passed. But every barrier, or "edge," of one thing is also the beginning of another. People once thought that airplanes would disintegrate when they reached the speed of sound. The speed of light may also be a border that only seems to be an obstacle.

Any civilization that has mastered space travel and has colonized another planet, as we someday will do with Mars, is also mastering the art of living in outer space without any planetary base. An interstellar ship will also be a complete space abode where a planetary environment can be duplicated. Huge arms rotating around a center point can generate artificial gravity. And interior spaces bigger than any sports superdome on earth will eventually be built. Ponds, trees, and even an artificial climate with rainfall can be created. The environment of the future space station can be so complete that it will be home to those who live there. Landing on other planetary bodies will then be useful but not necessary for the survival and happiness of these future space travelers.

We are at the beginnings of the era of space travel and space living. We have been to the moon, and we will return there to stay. We will send people to Mars, to the outer reaches of our solar system, and eventually toward other planets in other systems. It is an exciting adventure of the human spirit, the true achievement of living in space.

INDEX